Mary Baldwin College

The long walk on the front terrace is, just as it used to be - as any "old girl" will assuredly tell you — the favorite promenade of thousands of girls from all over the United States.

Lily Ripley Barnwell, class of 1881

Mary Baldwin College

Photographed by Daniel Grogan

Harmony House
Publishers - Louisville

Executive Editors: William Butler and William Strode
Library of Congress Catalog Number: 90-81398
Hardcover International Standard Book Number 0-916509-71-0
Printed in the Republic of Korea by Sung In Printing Company, LTD.
through Vivid Color Separation, New York, N.Y.
First Edition printed Spring, 1992 by Harmony House Publishers,
P.O. Box 90, Prospect, Kentucky 40059 (502) 228-2010 / 228-4446
Copyright © 1992 by Harmony House Publishers
Photographs copyright © 1992 by Daniel Grogan

This book or portions thereof may not be reproduced in any form without permission of Harmony House Publishers. Photographs may not be reproduced in any form without permission of Daniel Grogan.

BEAUTIFUL IN ELEVATION

"Everyone ought to have an alma mater" wrote Sociologist C.H. Cooley," a fellowship in exploring the social heritage and finding the interests and commitments that will set one on course toward a satisfying and productive life. The setting in which this takes place will become holy ground for the participants, who will return to it in later years for renewal of spirit through grateful recollection and occasional visits."

The scenes given in this volume will be more meaningful if the viewer comes to them with an overview of the Mary Baldwin College campus as a whole. We shall imagine the young woman in quest of a college that will be just the right one for her, getting her first glimpse of Mary Baldwin College in a row of cream-colored buildings putting one in mind of the public architecture of classical Greece: stately columns, porches, and walks. Her approach is from the east, and what she sees is the second tier of a tri-level campus, the lowest tier being partly obscured by intervening business and residential structures.

She passes under the railroad that for a century and more brought most of the boarding students to Staunton, and continues uphill on Coalter Street until she comes to the Woodrow Wilson Birthplace. She turns left on Frederick Street where the campus begins in a row of buildings of the same color she saw before, stretching on a level higher than the street itself for more than a couple of blocks. She passes in turn on her right the Pearce Science Center, Bailey Dormitory (a renovation of what was once the city hospital and where many alumnae were born), the Grafton Library, the Carpenter Academic Building, and the Administration Building where the present campus began with its erection in 1844, two years after the founding of what was then called the "Augusta Female Seminary." She will park her car here, although the campus actually extends across New Street in the form of several residences which have been adapted to college use.

The Administration Building is of great historical interest because it was once the entire College for nearly twenty years, providing dormitory space, classrooms, parlors, and administrative offices. At one time in the Civil War, the building was invaded by Union soldiers searching for food supplies whose clever hiding has been the theme of college dramatics ever since. On the porch of this building two Presidents, Woodrow Wilson in 1912, and Dwight Eisenhower in 1960, addressed crowded audiences. The event in 1912 devastated the boxwood and other shrubbery which had been the pride of the campus. As the visitor enters the building from the street, she ascends a long flight of steps guarded by two stone dogs, Ham and Jam.

Leaving the Frederick Street tier behind, she resumes her climb toward the stately mansions of the second level. She passes McClung Dormitory on her left, opposite which is the Carpenter Academic Building where most of the classes are held. Separating the two lowest levels is a grassy expanse stretching laterally across the entire breadth of the campus and lending spaciousness as if in compensation for the crowdedness of the first hundred years.

Just above this lawn is the second tier that first met the visitor's eye. She counts these buildings from west to east. First is Memorial Dormitory, behind which is the King Building with a basketball floor and swimming pool. East of Memorial is the oldest building on the campus — Hill Top Dormitory — which housed an elementary school before the Rev. Rufus Bailey came to Staunton in 1842 to found the Seminary which grew into Mary Baldwin College. The Wenger Building, containing the college post office and Miller Chapel, along with other facilities, is east of Hill Top. A patio separates Wenger from the Hunt Dining Hall, and the second tier is continued by Woodson and Spencer Dormitories, ending at Coalter Street.

The highest level calls for more steps. Most of this part of the campus was acquired from the Staunton Military Academy which went out of existence after a distinguished history of over a century. This property, acquired by Mary Baldwin in 1977, increased the total campus acreage to 54 acres. This part of the campus is still in process of development, but is well on the way. The President's Home occupies the summit. The Deming Fine Arts Building is one of Mary Baldwin's most attractive features. There is also the old mess hall of the Academy which is put to many purposes. A valuable legacy from the Academy is its athletic field and track, near which is the new gymnasium. Some buildings have been converted to administrative use and most of the business offices are here. Here, too, is the Sena Center for Career and Life Planning, with space reserved for later construction.

The Alumnae House is part of this top-level complex, and two dormitories. One of these provides housing for the girls in the early teens who are enrolled in the Program for the Exceptionally Gifted. The uppermost campus also contains what would be most astonishing to the student of an earlier period— some 500 parking spaces for cars, not one of which was available in 1930 when none of the students and few of the faculty owned cars.

Our visitor may leave the campus through the official entrance on Coalter Street. After all the climbing, she may wonder why she didn't begin her inspection at this level and be going downhill all the way. But that way she would have approached most of the buildings from the rear.

She has seen a campus unexcelled for its beauty, with a unity in architecture and color that suggests harmony and balance. The altitude affords vistas of the city in all directions and great chains of some of the oldest mountains in the world, as well as the charming hills of the fertile farmlands of the Shenandoah Valley. One recalls how the Psalmist found in what is elevated to be suggestive of what is ultimately unattainable and elusive, yet beckoning.

There is, of course, much more to a college than can be displayed in a photograph. What gives significance to any site is ultimately the human drama that is unfolding there. Mary Baldwin is an educational institution for women. Far fewer women attend the single-sex college than used to be the case; nevertheless, there are certain advantages. Male dominance is still in evidence in many aspects of the life on a coed campus, and women need to find a place for the special interests of their sex as well as full participation and leadership in the common life. The common element, at the same time, is not neglected, for women are increasingly filling roles that were long preempted by men, especially in the world of business.

The educational program that is going on at Mary Baldwin is an outstanding one. Some of the innovations have attracted widespread attention. In recent nationwide surveys, Mary Baldwin has been cited as one of the finest liberal arts colleges in the region. The faculty is well trained, the classes are relatively small; no one is a mere number. Admission standards select students from whom other students can learn. These students come from all over the country and abroad. One encounters a wide range of cultures and sub-cultures which challenge bigotry and provincialism. Nor are the associations limited to those of the 18 to 22 age range, for there are many women enrolled in the Adult Degree Program who return to the classroom later in life to complete their formal education. The Program for the Exceptionally Gifted brings girls in their early teens.

There is a full program of activities, with dramatics, music, painting, sports, publications, religion, and social service, to mention a few. Student Government is respected and effective. A good college will imbue its students with an idealism sorely needed in a competitive economy where one is tempted to short-circuit the rules. Business courses and computer science prepare students for the marketplace, but the liberal-arts college also offers encouragement for what Elizabeth Barrett Browning called "feeling out of sight for the ends of being and ideal grace." The college should foster the search for lasting aims that make life safe and just and satisfying. Mary Baldwin has had for many decades a highly successful honor system and a strong religious program to go along with the skills and wisdom in getting and spending.

"Beautiful in elevation, the joy of all the earth," wrote the Psalmist of his beloved Mount Zion, as we do, now, of Mary Baldwin College. The first part of this statment is one of fact; the second is the ambition and the prayer of all who love Mary Baldwin.

Dr. Thomas H. Grafton, Professor Emeritus
Mrs. Martha S. Grafton, Dean Emerita

ACKNOWLEDGMENTS

The idea for this book in celebration of Mary Baldwin College's 150th year came from the committee appointed to plan for 1992. But certain members deserve special thanks.

In their introduction, the Graftons speak of "all who love Mary Baldwin." Certainly no two people have ever shown more plainly their love of an institution than they, in countless ways for over sixty years.

Dr. Patricia H. Menk, Historian-in-Residence, has provided a chronology that heightens our appreciation for the pictures that follow.

And so, the Sesquicentennial Planning Committee hopes that you will derive much joy and pleasure from this glimpse of Mary Baldwin College, 1842-1992.

William C. Pollard
Chairman

MARY BALDWIN TIMELINE
By Dr. Patricia H. Menk — Professor Emerita of History

1842 "A Plan or Constitution of the Augusta Female Seminary" adopted by a "number of ministers and other gentlemen"; Rufus W. Bailey, who proposed founding the school, was named principal. Augusta Female Seminary held first session with about 50 pupils in a rented building on the corner of Court House alley and New Street. Later, removed to a house on Greenville Avenue. Among the pupils was Mary Julia Baldwin.

1844 Cornerstone of Main (Administration) Building laid "with appropriate religious ceremonies" completed on property belonging to the First Presbyterian Church on the corner of Frederick and New Streets. First Charter of Augusta Female Seminary granted by the Virginia State Legislature.

1846 Mary Julia Baldwin certified as completing her studies at Augusta Female Seminary. First May Day Celebration.

1855 Joseph Addison Waddell elected to the Board of Trustees. He served until 1914.

1855-56 Rev. Joseph R. Wilson served as principal and chaplain of Augusta Female Seminary. His son, Thomas Woodrow Wilson, was born at the Manse of the First Presbyterian Church, December 28, 1856.

1857 Annexes (two wings) added to the Administration Building. First boarding students accepted.

1863 Mary Julia Baldwin elected principal of Augusta Female Seminary, assisted by Agnes R. McClung. Miss Baldwin revised the curriculum with the assistance of Dr. W. H. McGuffey (University of Virginia). Miss Baldwin remained principal until her death on July 2, 1897.

1869-90 Brick House (McClung), Sky High, Hill Top, Covered Way, and the Chapel were built or acquired. Some time in the 1880s, Ham and Jam (once called Caesar and Pompey, Wellington and Blucher) appeared on the pedestals of the Frederick Street entrance to the Administration Building.

1882 Charlotte Kemper left the faculty to become a missionary in Brazil. She was the first of a long line of teachers and alumnae who entered the Christian mission field.

1890 W.W. King was appointed Assistant to Miss Baldwin. He was famous for his Red Head Club and his devotion to the students.

1892 *The Recorder* appeared "published by the Young Ladies of Augusta Female Seminary."

1893 Alumnae Association formed; Miss Nannie Tate was declared first president, assisted by Nellie Hotchkiss McCullough.

1894 Dr. Abel McIver Fraser elected to the Board of Trustees.

1895 The Virginia State Legislature, at the request of the Board of Trustees, changed the name of the school to Mary Baldwin Seminary "as an acknowledgment of their high appreciation of the valuable service and unparalleled success of the Principal for thirty-five years."

1896 First issue of *The Record* published by the Alumnae Association (later called *Alumnae Newsletter* and then *Alumnae Magazine*).

1897 Mary Julia Baldwin died; Ella Claire Weimar appointed principal.

1898 Observance of Mary Julia Baldwin's birthday began (origin of Founders' Day, so named in October 1941). First major campus expansion and building program under the direction of W.W. King. Two dormitories, Memorial and McClung, Academic, the Back Gallery, and Rose Terrace were built, acquired or remodeled; Mr. King made the decision that the new buildings would conform to the neoclassical style of Main and Hill Top and be painted white and cream.

1899 *Miscellany* (student literary magazine) first published; it was successor to *The Recorder*.

1910 *Bluestocking* (yearbook) begun.

1912 President-elect Woodrow Wilson spoke from the front porch of the Administration Building at a celebration honoring his fifty-sixth birthday. Class Day added to graduation ceremonies.

1916 Mary Baldwin Seminary approved by the State of Virginia as a junior college; Marianna Parramore Higgins appointed principal.

1919 Athletic Association founded.

1923 Mary Baldwin approved by the State of Virginia as a standard four year liberal arts college. Dr. Abel McIver Fraser named first president of Mary Baldwin College.

1924 First edition of *Campus Comments* (student newspaper).

1929 The Seminary (preparatory department) discontinued. Dr. L. Wilson Jarman named president of Mary Baldwin College. Elizabeth Pfohl (Campbell) appointed Dean of Women. Installation of Student Government Association; first president was Wilhelmina C. Eskridge (Mrs. G.A. Beard). First investiture of seniors with caps and gowns.

1930 Martha Stackhouse (Grafton) appointed Assistant to Dean Pfohl. In the course of the next thirty years she was Registrar, Academic Dean of the College, and Acting President on four occasions.

1931 Alumnae Office opened The Club for students.

1932 Mary Baldwin Honor Society founded.

1933 Mary Baldwin College became the first women's college to present the annual Algernon Sydney Sullivan Awards, sponsored by the Southern Society.

1933-34 First foreign exchange college students enrolled.

1934 Margaret Kable Russell, first woman and first alumna elected to the Board of Trustees.

1936 Mixed informal dancing allowed on Back Gallery.

1940 First Apple Day picnic. (Named Apple Day, October 1, 1946.)

1941 New Century Fundraising Campaign annnounced. A yearlong celebration in honor of the centennial year.

1942 Dedication of the William Wayt King Memorial Auditorium (Centennial Building).

1942-45 Curriculum adapted to wartime needs; faculty, alumnae and administrators joined the armed forces and support services. Students organized a Victory Corps.

1947 Dr. Frank Bell Lewis named third president of Mary Baldwin College. King Series (College/Community concert and lecture programs) began.

1948 College retreat, Chip Inn, near Stuart's Draft opened.

1951 Student Activity Building completed, later named in honor of Consuelo Slaughter Wenger.

1952 Eta Betas (student dining room waitresses) organized. Nannie Tate Demonstration School opened (Early Childhood Education). Mary Baldwin College became a charter member of the Virginia Foundation for Independent Colleges.

1953 Recreation Association sponsored the Scotch and Irish clans.

1954 Charles W. McKenzie appointed fourth president.

1955 Dedication of Rufus W. Bailey Dormitory. The Presbyterian Center for Guidance and Career Counseling located on the Mary Baldwin campus.

1956 First Mock Political Convention held; thereafter, held every four years.

1957 Synod of Virginia Campaign to benefit Mary Baldwin College, Hampden-Sydney and Union Theological Seminary. Dr. Samuel Reid Spencer elected fifth president of Mary Baldwin College.

1958 Trustees adopted Long Range Development Plan and approved a Capital Campaign; enrollment and campus area to be doubled. New Directions in Liberal Arts Program instituted; a major curriculum revision. Laurel Society organized. Honors Program for freshmen and sophomores begun.

1960 A ten year building program and campus expansion undertaken; Lyda Bunker Hunt Dining Hall (1961), Heating Plant (1962), Margaret C. Woodson Dormitory (1961), Samuel Reid Spencer Dormitory (1962), Martha Stackhouse Grafton Library (1967), Jesse Cleveland Pearce Science Building (1969); campus expanded to 16.5 acres. Market Street closed from Frederick to Academy Streets. Enrollment reached about 700. President Dwight D. Eisenhower spoke from the porch of the Administration Building (in honor of Woodrow Wilson). The President had lunch in King Building with 750 college members and guests. Ham and Jam restored in cast stone and bolted to their pedestals after pranksters broke them.

1961 Covered Way demolished as campus expanded across Market Street.

1962 Academic Year in Madrid Program inaugurated. Waddell Chapel razed after major structural weaknesses discovered. Wilson Memorial Terrace constructed on the site and dedicated, October 1963.

1962 U.S. - India Women's College Exchange Program instituted.

1965-66 First formal Self Study for the Southern Association of Colleges and Schools undertaken.

1965 Project Opportunity begun, a special relationship with secondary schools in Nelson County.

1967 Academic Summer in Oxford Program (now the Virginia Program at Oxford).

1967-68 Major curriculum revision, Challenge of a New Curriculum, begun.

1968 First Black student enrolled at Mary Baldwin College. Academic Year in Paris instituted.

1969 Dr. William Watkins Kelly became sixth president. In next seven years, compulsory chapel and church attendance ended; student social regulations moved from *in loco parentis* to an open-ended system complying with federal and state regulations and student-determined social parameters (1969-1977).

1970 Underclassmen allowed to bring automobiles to campus. Faculty and student representation on the Board of Trustees committees (non-voting). Mary Baldwin College's application for a chapter of Phi Beta Kappa acted on favorably: Lambda Chapter of Virginia Phi Beta Kappa installed April 26, 1971. Exchange Consortium program began. Committee on the Challenges of the Seventies.

1971-72 Ten million dollar capital fund campaign launched.

1973 Advisory Board of Visitors instituted; Governor's School for the Gifted (in Science) located at Mary Baldwin College (summer program).

1974 College charter revised to deformalize the relationship with the Presbyterian Church.

1976 Wenger Hall remodeled, dedicated as American Bicentennial Building. Laurel Circle of Omicron Delta Kappa installed at Mary Baldwin College, the first women's college in the United States to be authorized to have a circle. Dr. Virginia Laudano Lester elected seventh president. Board of Trustees approved the purchase of Staunton Military Academy property.

1977 Curriculum broadened to give career option preparation for the New Woman of the South (Arts Management, Business Management, Communications, Women's Studies, Social and Psychological Services).

1978 Adult Degree Program registered first students. Bailey Scholarship program announced. Year round use of the campus formalized with extensive summer programs.

1979 Covenant Agreement with Presbyterian Church. Kable Hall opened as a residence hall on upper campus.

1980 Exchange program with Doshisha Women's College, Kyoto, Japan begun.

1983 Deming Hall (Fine Arts Building) on upper campus dedicated.

1985 Rosemarie Sena Center for Career and Life Planning established. Dr. Cynthia Haldenby Tyson elected eighth president. Vision statement approved by the Board of Trustees. Program for the Exceptionally Gifted (PEG) begun, funded by a major grant from the Jesse Ball DuPont Foundation. Curriculum revision emphasized liberal arts core requirements, writing and mathematical competence, computer literacy and pre-professional training.

1988 Memorial Hall renovations completed. Dedication of Carpenter Hall (renovated Academic Building). Purchase of Staunton YMCA property.

1989 Health Care Administration and Christian Ministry Preparation Programs funded.

1990 Sesquicentennial Capital Campaign for $35,000,000 announced.

1991 Hill Top renovations completed. Founders' Day first event in yearlong celebration of Mary Baldwin College Sesquicentennial.

Charter Day on Page Terrace

Mary Baldwin is a college of physical beauty and distinction, known as such all over the land. I am proud of being an alumna of this great institution.

Mrs. Cordell Hull (Rosa Witz, Class of 1892)

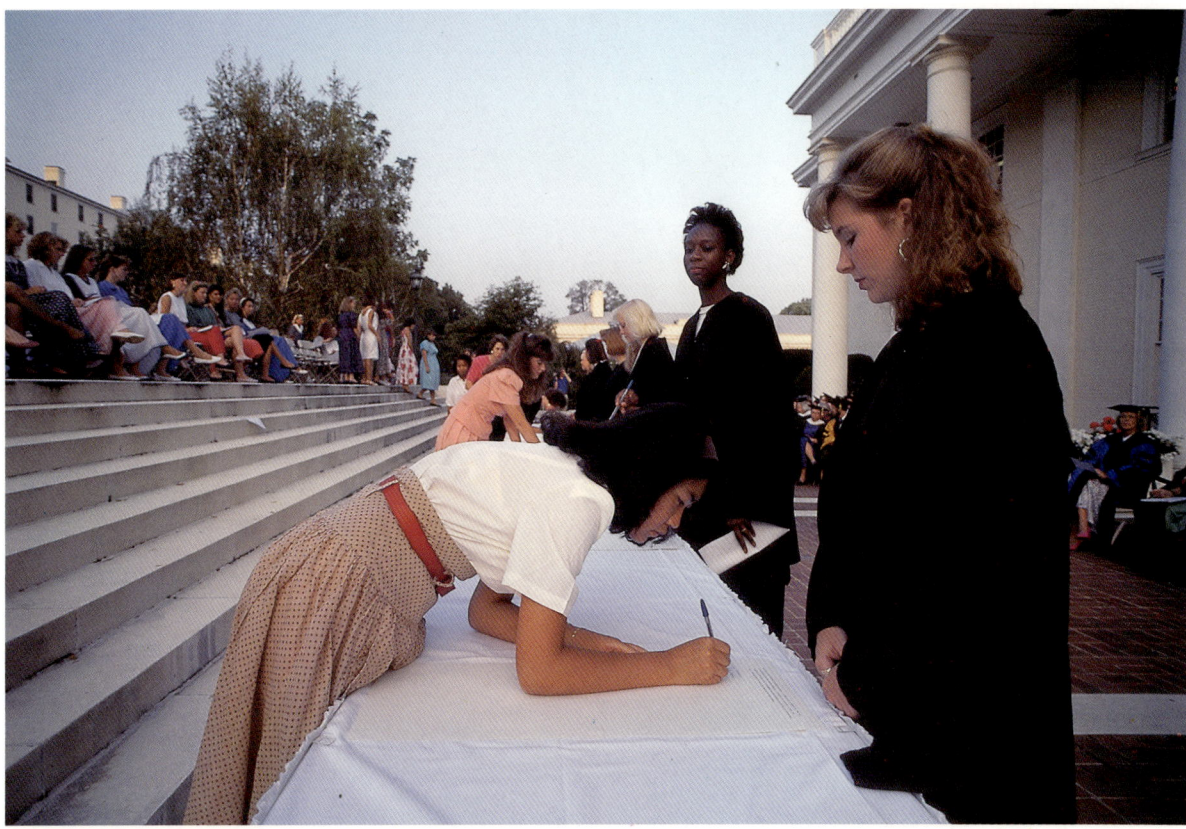

Overleaf; Martha Stackhouse Grafton Library

33

The Graftons

Institutions for the instruction of young ladies abound throughout the country, and there may be others as deserving of public confidence as this, but I have never known such a school. It is as near perfection in my judgment as it is possible for human wisdom to make it.

Dr. Joseph R. Wilson, former Principal, 1868

Memorial and Hilltop

Deming and Kable

Lyda Bunker Hunt Dining Hall

The scene in and around the institution was most attractive. The terraced yard with its lawns and fountains, and the portico filled with flowers . . . were fit surroundings for the halls of the institution, which were decorated with exceptional good taste.

Republican Vindicator, June 11, 1875

Administration Building

Ham and Jam

Around Staunton

Presidential Portraits

The achievement of Mary Julia Baldwin was the product of a strong, clear, practical intelligence, of unusual courage and of religious faith, completely devoted to the realization of an ideal of woman's education . . . for her achievement through her school, Miss Baldwin deserves recognition as one of the great women educators of the country. With complete justice, the school was later renamed the Mary Baldwin Seminary in her honor and stands today as Mary Baldwin College, a monument to her memory.

Dr. Mary Watters in *The History of Mary Baldwin College 1842-1942*

Coalter Street Entrance

Bailey Dormitory and Pearce Science Center

Gypsy Hill Park

Downtown Staunton

Grave of Mary Julia Baldwin, Thornrose Cemetery

Woodrow Wilson Birthplace Museum

Blue Ridge Parkway

During our recent tour of the South, we perpetually heard of the Augusta Female Seminary at Staunton, Virginia as one of the most deservedly celebrated schools for girls in that region . . . The Seminary . . . is situated in one of the most beautiful and healthful towns in the Valley of Virginia.

In *The Journal of Education*, Boston, 1881

We aim first to prepare each child to live in time with a wise reference to eternity.

Board of Trustees in *Address to the Citizens of Augusta County*, September 1842

Christmas Cheer

Junior Dads

Apple Day

83

The mind must think. Why may she not as well be wise as frivolous? Why may she not as well be devoted to literature as to fashion? Why may not the conversation of mixed companies which occupies so large a share of our time and attention, be rational, literary, and improving, instead of being, as it too often is, vain, unprofitable, and dissipating?

Founder Dr. Rufus W. Bailey in
Daughters at School

Homecoming

Commencement

The ascending tiers of school girls on either side of the orchestra, like rose-buds of varied hue studded in a huge bouquet, seemed to perfume the air all around with their fragrance . . .
The benediction pronounced . . . the girls sprang like birds from their bowers to congratulate each other, the boys in adoring wonder stood spellbound, the old sighed over days long since gone by and, amid this glorious melee of earthly joys, seizing our hat and shaking off the reverie of the hour, we bade adieu to one of the brightest scenes of our life.

In the *Valley Virginian*, May 22, 1884

MARY BALDWIN COLLEGE

Engraving of Augusta Female Seminary, 1860

*A brief look back through photographs
from the college archives*

Rufus William Bailey, Founder

No portrait or photograph of Miss Baldwin exists; she would permit none to be made.

Dr. Mary Watters in *The History of Mary Baldwin College 1842-1942*

Agnes McClung, Head of Seminary Boarding Department

The Art Studio, 1900

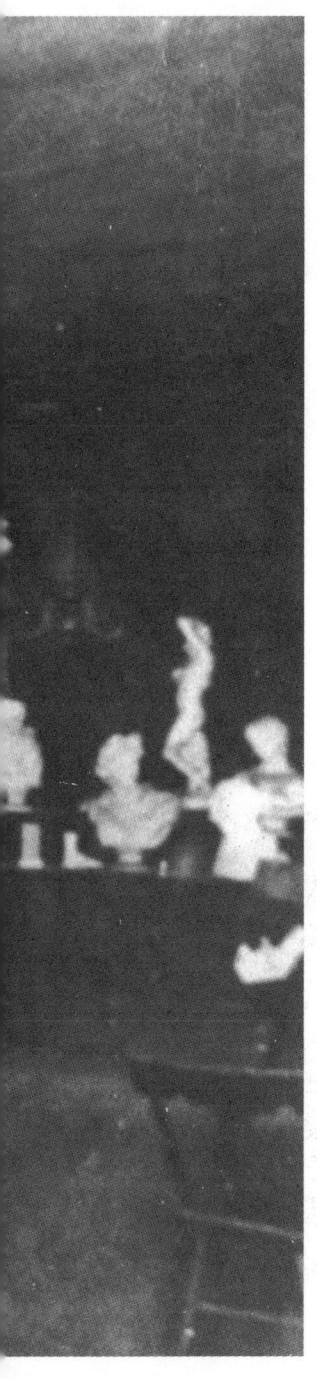

Tennis Group, 1900

Golf Class, 1904

Class Day ceremonies, 1920

Alumnae Luncheon, 1925

Class Day, 1930s

Garden Party, 1920s

Getting mail, 1935

The Dining Hall, 1935

Basketball in the mid-30s

Chip Inn, late 1940s

Field Hockey, 1950

Mary Baldwin girls arrive by train in Staunton station, 1940

Apple Day, 1960

Time to sign in, 1960